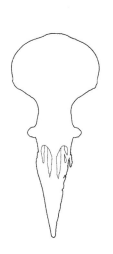

Dead Birds Of New Zealand
© Christian Czaniecki / Cathexis Northwest Press

No part of this book may be reproduced without written permission of the
publisher or author, except in reviews and articles.

First Printing: 2020

Paperback ISBN: 978-1-952869-01-3

Cover art by C. M. Tollefson
Designed and edited by C. M. Tollefson

Cathexis Northwest Press
cathexisnorthwestpress.com

DEAD BIRDS

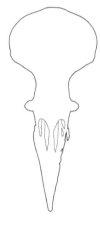

OF
NEW ZEALAND

CHRISTIAN CZANIECKI

THANK YOU TO THE COLLECTED GROUP OF PEOPLE WHO HAVE SUPPORTED MY PURSUIT OF FINDING SOME KIND OF SIMPLE BEAUTY IN WORDS OVER THE LAST WHO KNOWS HOW MANY YEARS.

SPECIAL THANKS TO JUDY COOPER, CHRIS MALLOS, MORGAN LINFORTH, JOSH PAKI, AND THELMA KARAITIANA

A Truncated Genealogy of the Ocean

All of the world's birds
have gathered to watch
another bird dive into

the white cresting
of a wave like shell
fragments blown in
a circle of wind across

the wet glass of
a perfectly drawn eye

Who put those
balloons here
this was supposed
to be

                                     a funeral

Every dead thing
         is the reintroduction

of carbon

                 nobody needs
                 into
                         the ecosystem

The alternative is living
                 forever
which

                 could be

                                       worse.

I could point you to
a poem about life
or death but we are
in one & it's about to
be full of the bones
of so many things all
of them blue as a thorn
songs no one remembers
all the bones laid out
in a diagram shaped like
the universe ready to
        explode

In a closed

                              system
                    nothing
is ever

          lost

                         The most

unfortunate
thing
about living

                              it never

          ends

FIRST IT WAS FUNNY, THEN IT WAS A FIRE

One of the things
I wrote down was
meant to be funny

I can't remember
what it was the words
turned into an animal

it wasn't a wolf & when
it opened its mouth
it exploded into light

& marbles made of
whale bones I mailed
all the pieces I could

back to Chris & asked
him to give them as
gifts in case I never

leave New Zealand I'm
being silly it's going
to be night forever

unless I open my
eyes I wish this bag
wasn't over my head

I can see right through
it but it's messing up
my hair & this is the

season when things

14

nest in there & so
many things are

dying everywhere
all the time   That
building was

a forest the lobby
is painted like a
forest the people

inside sell paper
towels and stationary
I started writing on

the lobby floor in
chalk & the whole
building went up

in flames I don't
know if there was
laughing or screaming

at least part of what
I wrote was funny
the last word was
madness

I CAME TO NEW ZEALAND AND DIED POLITELY, BECAUSE THAT'S HOW YOU DO THINGS IN NEW ZEALAND

Most of the birds here have

done that too

There is a story when Cook sailed past Aotearoa he heard
bird song from two kilometers away.

This is of course bullshit

The kilometer wasn't established until 1816, years after
Cook discovered a land already inhabited by people considered
too dark to appreciate the blessings of a land without
the intervention of white men and their white god.

Every place
I've ever   been
                    sounds the   same
a grind   of bones   and industry
          the gravity of aliveness   people
swaying   like a forest
that suddenly   decided to move

occasionally a bird

Does it matter that my bones are hollow if I am half buried
in sand. In the morning people light candles hold a vigil
I blow them out shaking my wings in great silver sheets
silhouetted by the more silver moon that never leaves the
sky while I am here

I'm not

                                    dead

                                            yet

Don't be silly   says an old woman

                                                            taking

a struck match

                                            to the wick

of a   votive

Everything here is dead

Every island, yes every island, yes

Every island is   sinking or
the ocean is rising   does it matter if [you]
      are flying or the sky

                is fall(ing)

when [you] find [you]rself inside
    a   cloud   wet most(ly)

blind   like being   born without

          the part where life begins.

Everything worth having is worth selling for more than you paid
I didn't notice when my heart was made into a commodity who can
understand what it is that makes a thing real enough to be bought.

Very near here there is   a   place
          where(?)   [we] buried
      fish to make them grow
             feet   smooth(ed)
the black earth with
        [our] p(s)alms &
washed away
        streaks of mud
      lines in the dawn made of pure love

                  across
our faces.

[We] came
back

a day later and there was a pile of silver feathers & piles of rocks shaped
like a nest. Neither of [us] knew it then but the ground was full of bones.

ALL CITIES HAVE A WOLF, OR THEY SHOULD

At some point every
city becomes a place
more forgetting
than living
Where did I put
my left eye Did
I really need it
It was made
out of amber
always pointing
towards the past
Isn't it the whole point
not to need
anything you can't
carry to the fire
like a beacon
a ghost hopelessly
lost from its haunting
on the hillside
overlooking your house
after you burned
it to the ground
& moved to the forest
to become a wolf
wear a wolf's skin
making wolf sounds
until a woman
asks what you are
doing in her garden
stealing toys
from her children
and eating only
red vegetables

THEY SHOULDN'T BE ALLOWED TO CALL THAT A TACO

I was absolutely
right to believe
that I couldn't
survive this thing
without changing
because every

time I cum the world

is worse than it
was before

Let me stop
thinking about
my dick, it was
mostly ornament-
al until I quit
opening parts
of my arm
to insert parts of

god

my veins

illustrated as
displeasure
in blue lines

as septic & beautiful
as every bird

that died frozen

having flown the
wrong way or too
far the right way

I don't have any
claim to your
neck but that
doesn't make it
less of a possess-
ion to my mouth

Part of my body
is painted black

darker than ash

or sadness or
the frozen eye
of a bird darker
than rocks
arranged in

circles to line

up with the moon
the sun to read the sky
better

sacrifice the innocent

I didn't have
anything to do
with creation if
I had it would
have been bright-
er and not as

long the planet

or the sun has
moved & the rocks
don't line up

with anything use-
ful I had nothing
to do with the
platypus but I'll

take the credit

22

STRUGGLING WITH METRIC CONVERSION

I don't know how many feet
it is until the edge of the world,
all the signs are in meters
& the light reflecting off puddles
in oily pinks and blues   collecting

the lonely parts of people on
their way to here leaving them
before they step
off the broken white
                bone   edge
into the darkness between now
& everything else

In the empty spaces
the outlines of teeth as sharp
& white as childbirth   warble glimmer
with the silver ambling of stars as
they are eaten from parts of the sky
parts of the night that hold the hunger
of imaginary animals & you & I
having been here before for nearly
forever

toss little flames into the
reflections that are shaped like
our lives and poured into a bottle

An improvised ship
a time capsule
Little bird skeletons
walk up next to you
& ignore me

23

Perfect sets off bones
flapping their white branches with no
leaves like trees that died but won't
fall to the wind

You ask me if all dead
things are so prideful I
shrug and fall   backwards laughing
You were the one
that told us we were dead and it would
be amazing

24

I Can Assure You That No One Fucking Cares

I heard arguably
the saddest words
ever.

I said them
then I forgot
bummer.

Cats forget their kittens
after a few weeks
a tree gives zero fucks

about the leaves it sheds
nature has a humility for
disregarding the beautiful

that I've never fully appreciated.

Have I told you how I invented
the perfect darkness then sold
the patent. I was still drinking.

Mistakes were made.

I wanted to ask someone
to tell me the truth but I don't
know what time it is in the

place where people still bother
with that. Can I tell you how
to love something forever

it's similar to floating in

a still dark part of the ocean
lean back try not to struggle

& then drown.

Nonlinear Expression of Time

It's a shame I wasn't born a fish
the passage of time seems less
significant underwater when you
aren't drowning

I keep appearing from the future
leaving myself half smoked
cigarettes & cryptic notes
(run) (you don't like boats)

I smoke the cigarettes & ignore
the notes I don't know how future
me can be any more trustworthy
than right now me

I didn't know anything about time
travel when this started I still don't
I wanted someone to believe I was
& then die believing that

So I resisted texting you from 16
hours in the future to tell you I
loved you because when you caught
up to me I would be running in circles

Chain smoking on the prow of a ship
writing missives into folded napkins
& watching the ink diffuse out into
the shape of spiral galaxies

No one told me to do this
Future me says it was raining
Future me is a liar

I'M HERE UNTIL WHENEVER

I was or am having
a tea on Courtney Place
& they ask
if I want milk &
I look at them
I hold coins like
they are a novelty
or a riddle & they know
I don't belong here

DEAD BIRDS OF NEW ZEALAND

Take a moment to consider the rose bush
as a colonial construct   Adolescence
as a function of western excess   Gender

There are more bone(s) in your
hand than there are rose(s)
I made that up there are 22
bones in your hand & infinite
roses

Wellington harbor was shaped
by a taniwha or a volcano
depending then the British
Every one agrees with that
I was shaped by sex   privilege
& probably heroin
Definitely

DON'T BELIEVE THE PLANTS WHEN THEY TELL YOU THEY HAVE YOUR BEST INTERESTS IN MIND

Did you see there was
                    & then there wasn't
a coffin
                    shaped like
a   bird
                        & full of birds

        Should something

like that be buried
                or burned

                                        Probably both
            Smoke
                        stops rising
        when no one

is watching it
                        Plants
that move towards the sun
                do so in
secret

Lying about where they will be

        One day a bud
the next day a balloon

                                    so blue
it's dangerous to be alone with

                No one knows what

happens after you

                                                    die

take that to mean
                        nothing here
            is worth
coming back for
                                    Smile more

the birds will be

            alive when we
bury them
                        dead when they burn

When I was young I was afraid
of everything I got older and realized
I was being overly conservative
Have you ever slept long enough
for your hair to change colors
A tree gone green to red
as a moment so bright that it breaks
every heart in existence
When I was a boy I was terrified
the trees were growing into my room
to carry me away. Every place I'd ever
seen was wonderful until I got there
& it was full of people or worse
I was alone

I Have a Wind

I have the most human
of delusions that every time
I flap my arms,
covered as they are

in silver feathers

the rest of the world has
been up to nothing but
waiting for wind.

Please be proud
      of me
I made an art

      I could make
one for you   if only
      I could find
a way to   (~~give a shit~~)
            not find my way
into the ocean.

Like falling to avoid
an oncoming car
its headlights cracking
the night apart over
a wet ghost
of the moon reflecting
like a man in a glowing
sheet practicing a haunting.

Why is the ocean
        so empty
in the parts   I fall
        into just by
                    luck
you would assume
        I'd land on someone

and they would love me

The secret to becoming a bird
is never telling anyone that you can
fly. No one wants to know that you
have a secret after they have heard
it and can't have it for their own.

I only wanted to know
        if the sky

                            was the same
when you were
        in it
If I could   do it
        again   I would
have prayed
        for something else.

There is a woman wearing a hat with one
of my feathers in it. That means almost
nothing, but it is beautiful.

PRIVATE FUNERAL FOR MR. Z

I only ever really wanted
to have a name that meant
something completely absurd
My parents called me Christian
Checkmate

Every bone is out of place
until it stops moving, human
hair has the same tensile
strength as steel at the same
diameter. Everything blue is
moving away from you or
could be

When I was a kid I thought
I'd fall in love & stay that
way forever, now that I
probably will, it seems less
useful. When I hide under
the coffee table my friends
pretend they can't see me

They have all come with red
flowers and handfuls of dirt
they drop them on the table
in a heap, say a few words,
and go to eat all of the food
in my apartment and pick
through my possessions.

We do this monthly & then
go back to our lives quiet

& ordinary as the green
expanse of summer
a single point in the distance
that knows fall will
make it more beautiful by
making it not itself

No one ever thanks the air
for being invisible. We should.
Can you imagine your breath
as an expression of color.
Sometimes my friends leave
me a plate of food before they
go, sometimes they lay down
beside me.

SHAMANISM AND KUMERA (IT'S LIKE A SWEET POTATO)

What I'm trying to say is that even
in the dark I can see my breath
calling out to you I leave the window
open so it can take on a shape

I woke up and there were frozen
silver flowers growing from the sill
part of the road north from Wellington washed away last night

The flowers were where you were
I was happy

the ocean is everywhere
here It needs to pick a side
I'm American & I can't understand
things that aren't polarized

a woman was

found dead bludgeoned
to death with
a bottle in her yard
it stopped being summer

maybe the flowers I've been breathing
towards you will wrap you in linen & pull

you close enough for me to taste
the patina from your lips
Everything has promised to stay
alive the whole day tomorrow

it's going to be a big day

the google home page just says fuck
a forest watched itself turn into canoes
the ocean just picked a side
the entire world just said fuck

IT'S THE CLITORIS OR THE END OF CHILDHOOD

Does anyone really know what happened
to the rest of our childhood

        there was youngness   like a tooth
             we were wiggling free
in our mouths
                then it fell out
      & we
immediately regretted

            not having it there

It's like there was endless wonder

        fumbling in the dark

with someone else's
        buttons and sinking
a hand into tight

                    denim spaces

      blue & grain soft

      like a mouth lined

                  with skin & cotton

interpreting breath and body pressure
like abstract art or an ancient language
        erased by music

This far is good   That far is not

Then POOF

               the clitoris

      Confetti

Now everything is confined
dollars per square foot
work parties
matching a vase
to your neighbors

        expectations

pretending that your hands remember
what to do when faced
with an unfamiliar

       body

This is a penis

              faster poof
     less confetti

If you give dolphins or boys

    a mirror they will
    stare at their junk.

Did you find the place
      where we lose things

        can we lose

Justin Bieber there it's a shame when good Canadians turn American

Take your shirt off

      & poof

you're an asshole

Take this pill to stop your head
            from exploding

               it will also make you grow
          feathers

There are only two solutions
to a broken heart

Both of them are human sacrifice

Your neighbor criticizes your

                    rose bush(es)
                    you scream into

a vase and mail it to him

Someone in the office found a clitoris
they weren't supposed to

      & poof

everyone is wearing black
robes   carrying knives & torches

I'm not going to anymore parties
with you

I'm staying home to binge watch
                        dolphin videos
            and scream
                        until it turns to

            confetti

ALL OF THE STARS, ALL OF THEM

I saw a woman from a distance
in the square off Cuba Street
in her belly she was carrying all
of the world's stars round like the
future or the most perfect expression
of gravity as if any moment she
might lay down and put her feet
on a bench and scream 10,000
birds flying forth from her pussy

I have a sketchbook that lights
itself on fire every time I close it
burning in pastels so bright they
can only exist in complete madness
& making the rubbing plastic noises
of crickets when they are afraid
When I tried to draw her
my pen curled like a snake
& drowned itself in a puddle

I didn't know how to tell her
she was holding everything
I wanted & am terrified of
There is only so much time
for making things that might
unmake themselves later
I've never wanted to love
or hurt something enough
to bring it into the now

AMERICA FROM A DISTANCE

I am going to be friends
with my neighbor's cat
until one of us decides
to eat the other

Hunger is a way to want
with a purpose the simplest
        kind of prayer
               the body says
 to the mind
       & repeats

I just saw the only cloud

that looks like   nothing
then it turned into
madness

How did the day get long
      enough to seem
              like a good
        idea

I had 7 new feathers today
         part of their purpose
             was to be counted

People have been moving
rocks between themselves
& the ocean for millennia

It only took me a week to
learn to

                                        fly

In my country people won't
                    give up their guns
but everyone else has to
                    give up porn

Americans look just as stupid
from the sky as they do
in person.

I finally flew high enough to see
                    God
            We didn't speak

I haven't learned to land

yet

Children think
                    that most adults are full
of shit

That is why people keep shooting them

At some point
                    even my heart
            is going to stop
                                beating

44

I left it in a box
                hooked up to a car battery
the chimpanzee
      guarding it only knows
                              three words
        He is better
              at praying
      than I will ever be

The ocean keeps moving closer

Americans are
      the only ones
      who know
      why

                & lie about it

Someone put a flower
            next to a dead child
      no one
            had ever seen
            anything
so red

If we lie still long enough
the grass will grow up
around us in castles
nearly tall enough to save
us from the ocean

It's not really my heart in that box

Anzac Day 2018

There is a series of rocks
& a faceless woman
a sign to remember
the war

We do this in the U.S. too
remember the dead
build things for them
& largely forget that
we are bleeding

BEAUTIFUL

The most beautiful woman

i've ever
seen
decided
to be so
& so
she was
rail thin
hiding
her cock
like it was
a tag
on a suit
she might
return

curved like
the night
wearing
a dress
made of linen
the color
of the sea
printed with
a human
skeleton
as if she wanted
you to see
into her
to see how
her bones had
been burnt

i wanted
to bite
her throat
leave marks
my teeth
on the arcing
shelves of her
hip bones
know
exactly if
that fire
was like

the one that I know

Capricious-

ROOTED FROM THE ITALIAN WORD CAPRICCIO WHICH IN TURN DERIVES FROM CAPO "HEAD" AND RICCIO, THE WORD FOR "HEDGEHOG". SOMEONE WHO SHUDDERED IN FEAR THEN WAS SAID TO HAVE A "HEDGEHOG HEAD"

Given enough time to realize
the inevitable and unenviable
end of their choices even
flowers stop moving towards
the sun   sprout   rise skyward
wilt

I saw a young girl drunk & fallen
into a puddle of her own vomit
ringed by her friends crooning
birds shaped like trumpets
the girls face half lovely & childish
half covered in her insides
I bought her a liter of water
a pile of napkins because
that would have happened
to me alone

I have been piling pieces
of glass and bird feathers
like a totem in the park
by my flat   The sun
hits it in the morning &
everything turns to

bright sky
bright water
like it had
electrified

49

the most perfectly
blue ever

Almost immediately
after it falls over & the world
is still the world but no one
is alone again

There is no good left
in the world
                        but
            not
                                    to worry
there isn't really
            any bad
                            either

There is nothing like
a good oversimplification
Apples are essentially a sex
organ. I'll leave that there for
you

One hundred times in a row
the sky makes me feel small
just once it doesn't & I keep looking

You told me once you would love
me forever   one day
that will mean the same thing
to both of us

On the same day I think
everything around us will
turn to stars

Sometimes I'm afraid
                                I'm not
           going to get
what
               I want
Sometimes that I will lose
           what
                             I have

Everything here is mine
not by force or right or need
but the ardent wanting inside
everything that lets gravity
pull stars into the center
of the universe   You
said one thing

          & I swallowed
all existence
I opened
                           my mouth
& the world
               went blind

You know this is just what
you wanted I'm wrapped up
in bed sheets & lost
flailing & drowning in linen
& the fear that only means

the world will end differently
than I want it to

I had just told a train it's velocity
was insignificant.   it wasn't

Outside the rain is more
or less involved in everything
hard at work making all of it
less beautiful   there are 40
geese
                         that don't
belong in the middle
              of the road
facing
                         each other
              staring into

Their partners tiny geese
eyes

Then they explode from left
to right except the two in the
center that make geese noises
fly off

I walk past all the feathers
spread like confetti
Somebody won this war
most didn't

I'm still
                        wrapped
            in sheets
like a child
                                 practicing
being a ghost

In a minute the wind will
blow
                        I'll either
                explode
or fly off with you

FIRMLY TIED TO NOTHING

I had meant to hold
a little longer   tighter
vines the remnants
of an abandoned church
aloft   a portent
of something like god
then of man

the vines remembering
the red bricks
once belonged to them & the earth
swallow them
& recede

I said I would come back from the far side of the world
imagine a different me in a different place
in a darkness so complete that all of the living
things inside have been born without eyes

I intend to keep
at least a part of
my word

the sun is in a predictably blue place in the sky
even if the warmth of it seems lost

NO SURPRISES HERE

I have always been a bird
I can't say I'm surprised
everyone has a name
for who they are what
they are

There are missives as
hollow as dog fur quiet
like the long shadow
of the moon realizing
it doesn't belong in
the afternoon

My mother told me she
still loved me my father
I don't remember
what happened next I
could hear anything

over the crunch of bones
the earthy taste of hair
and blood

I swallowed
a mouse

I'D NEVER KILL ANYTHING IF I STAY WELL FED

Don't keep the mob waiting
all of the roses are crisis actors
they don't even have a scent

We had places for our terror
when we were young
now we are afraid even
when
the lights are on

I knew a woman once
who would get goose-
bumps like her body
was speaking to me

in braille I don't know
how she was so
certain I wanted to
hurt her That's a lie

Are you going to finish that
can I bite the soft parts
on either side
of your hip bones

Every body speaks wanting
more clearly than it
means to like dressing
before a window &

only remembering shame
when someone looks in
& there is no

56

hiding anything

needle scars
cut marks building
in thickness up to
a pain so meaningful

you covered it with
a compass Maybe the
next one will mean what
all the ones before could
not

There is nothing unique

your pain There are
several people walking
over hot coals there are
several more holding a child

waiting for their turn

I WANT TO BE A GOOD BOY

1.
I want to be a good boy
I want to be a useful human

I'm beginning to wonder
am I one of the pieces
of machinery left over
after an engine
is taken
apart and put back
together better without
me. I'll be the best
piece in the box
of discarded things

2.
I have a secret if I tell
you can I stay here longer
There is a point in history
when dogs chose comfort
over freedom.

3.
I know I said I invented
the darkness
I did
in the way that Europe
invented God. It had
existed in one form or
another I just made it
a weapon

4.

Have I already told you
the story of how Christian
wrote a poem & no one
noticed for 20,000 years
until the glacier around his
body melted.

5.

The first drink was amazing
the first drink to get out
of bed wasn't Everything
with water balloons was
amazing

6.

Strawberries know
their worth enough to strangle
everything near them. Every
berry is a tacit approval
of murder. I had so many
of those growing up in the West

7.

I'd tell you now
but we have all committed
to killing each other
until we get to the part
of the movie where we look
back and it was all worth it

8.
Do you remember the boy
you loved in your youth
Neither does he
it & become someone less
carved out of wood and more
worn down by the rain

9.
A sound is carved by a river
a fjord is carved by a glacier
Both are
versions of the water pushing
me out to sea

Feed me rocks and seeds and let me alone to die

People have taken   to
throwing rocks   &
birdseed at me   I

I went to the park and buried my arm to the wrist in the wet shadow of the earth
like an ostrich or some distorted plant left over from the Pliocene

Have been bathing   in
a fountain   the
water sliding off   of
me into oily   rain-
bows flattened   out
smoke as parts   of
the sky wash   out
of my feathers   which
is to say I   probably deserve   the
stones.

I intended to say for 7 days until I saw god or the curvature of the earth, an hour later
I was eating dumplings on Boulcott Street fumbling chopsticks with my left hand

I haven't wanted   to
fly in weeks   the
sky is so vast   even
god occasionally   loses
itself that explains   a
lot of what happens   when
words mean less   than
ever when they   are
said all at once   the
dogs all howl   in
agony power   goes
out everywhere   for

3 seconds

My right hand held towards the sky, black mud drying brown on my skin
I am a failure

BIRDMAN OF ALCATRAZ

Why have you never
asked me what it's like
to be
a bird

There are walls
throughout the sky
every cloud looks
like something until it
looks like something
you want   more

Every time I hear
someone says God
I am a child again
& I am afraid
the sky is full
of something not heaven
I learned
to fly

& wanted to pull out
my feathers like undoing
threads holding the
wings like transplant limbs
onto my back ash blue
& foreign my body
rejecting me more
than the wings

Every dog wants to be
a wolf until it wants
to be held I wanted to
be a boy again until
I wanted to be undone

63

DEAD BIRDS IN THE SHAPE OF A CLEFT NOTE

I should have just lied
the shape of the moon
does that to us all the time

There was no more bird
sound & the sky was so
lonely it died from it

Dead starlings like grey
and brown stones formed
a cleft note of bird corpses
in a field so green it moved
in waves

I pulled my coat tighter
around my feathers I've never
wanted to be anything enough
to be the last of them

DID YOU MEAN FOR ME TO ENTER, DIFFERENTLY

I was not
I wasn't sure
if you wanted
for me to peck
at your window
so I flew
away
before you could
open
invite me
into
                                        your hidden

portion of everywhere
your walls

tapestries of elephants

a life sized sun

dangling
how
did that fit
over
your bed why
didn't I
wait a little longer   for you
          to rise & keep me
                              as a pet

Do you look
out
into the sky
when
the wind taps
against
the glass

I've never
lived in a tree
this long.

Clouds will never love you back the way a house cat will

I started to discuss my feelings
towards direct sunlight
lonely thing feeding &

burning because he can
because it is the only way
he knows to love

The gathering of clouds
more sympathetic than I
would have imagined

Watch me turn into a giraffe
they said All things can see
a dog's soul coruscating

bounding flashlights running
over the earth like their joy
will discover a place or a body

that's been lost Humans they say
are not so luminous They asked
if I looked down when I flew.

Only now that the sky is so
empty They shared their sadness
for the last birds dying &

turned their effusive billowing
elsewhere towards a more appropriate
audience with the dogs howling in

unison at the appearance of the low
winter moon molting lizard skins
not quite out of the eye line of the sun

EVERYTHING, MAYBE?

I just realized that everything
wait
   what could I possibly know
     about that
     I have only a handful
of bird feathers
        & a scar
the color of the wind
   to show for all the years
of my life.

You learned how to know me the way
I wanted. Afraid &
impressed that I could feel

enough to
circuitously I meant to say I love you
or at least the parts of you that loved
me back, the rest is useless to me.

There was just a moment
     ago
an owl perched on
the chair
across from me
his head turned completely
around &
he exploded into confetti

             the sound
the night makes   when
   you need
       ~~aloneness~~ (something?)
& immediately regret
   ~~having it.~~
   (Everything)

SPIZELLA ARBOREA

America hasn't killed all
of its birds yet but it will

A rejection of science has
lead to the failure of thermo-
dynamics in practice &
sparrows have been falling

at my feet like sputtering mud
stained engines. Charcoal
trying to burn under
water. I've been collecting

them in my bag & carrying
them around like chirping
ghosts feeding them bits
of my hands & my heart.

Whispering forbidden bird
songs to them. All the music
is owned & the sparrows can't
afford to buy back their own

voices from iTunes. I'm
going to take them west
to the desert painted in
the colors of weathered

skin golden a tooth
& scarred by the wind &
persistence of living.
I take the birds one by